CRIMES OF THE IRANIAN REGIME

Authored by

Ibrahim Ahmad

Contents

Introduction

This is an important topic which needs to be fully addressed and it will be made apparent to the reader that this Iranian Regime is dangerous to all of mankind, is the true "axis of evil" which is constantly plotting against both the enemies and so called friends. This is because it is ruled by a group of hardcore hypocrites who are masters in deception, lying, betrayal and oppression. These are the clergy of Iran who wears the religious cloaks but carry the hearts of devils. These are a people who have a very dark history and have no shame whatsoever in carrying out the most abominable crimes.

We have made the discussion very light based on actual unchallenged factual information. This treatise is a summary of the evil crimes of this regime. Anyone with a sound human conscious, moral ground, concern for humanity, mutual respect, and self-integrity will not co-operate with this regime, nor support it, nor aid it in any manner whatsoever. Rather it can be said that the one with the sound healthy heart who is guided by truth will fight this evil with all his might, and this evil is Iran which represents "Ignorant Regime of Arrogance and Nefariousness"(IRAN).

This is a regime that the whole world has united against in condemning its terrorist designs, its propagation of terrorism, and its exportation of terrorism, its logistical support of terrorism, and its ideological support of terrorism.

 It is incumbent upon those who have engagement with this evil regime to be on alert and not be deluded and deceived by them lest they regret it later.

This is a regime which needs to be immediately dismantled, defeated in totality both its ideological and military roots. Only when it is entirely defeated will the bloodshed end in the Middle East and Afghanistan, Pakistan and in many other countries. And if this is not stopped then it will carry on.

Terrorism is all its forms is evil and can never be justified in taking the life of innocent civilians who are caught up in a war. Yet Iran is the biggest actor and supporter of the merciless killings in Syria and elsewhere. Bloods of millions has been spilt by this evil Regime, so the patience with it has ended and there is no chance for history to repeat itself. This regime will end as this is the destiny of every oppressor who has taken unlawful blood, killed innocent babies and mothers in the lands of Iraq and Syria. Iranian terrorism has increased rapidly in the last few years through its complete support for its proxies in Syria, Lebanon, Iraq, and

Yemen which has destabilized the region and led some nations on the brink of poverty. This is a threat not only to the security of the Middle East but it has wider implications and it's in an international security threat. Iran condoned the despicable criminal chemical weapons deployment by the Syrian regime this is clear proof that the Iranian Khomeinism is the worst case of terrorism.

It is not possible to collate all the evidences against Iranian Terrorism since it will literally run into thousands of pages in the most condensed form. Iran is inspired by the devil and this is why it is representative of everything evil, from its roots to its policies- all are oppressive and evil.

Links with Al-Qaeda and ISIS (Daesh)

Contrary to popular belief Al-Qaeda, Daesh and the Taliban are all pro-Iran agents. And they carry the same goal although it may be appear that they have doctrinal differences in their creed. This is the case, but they are never true to their creed or their country. These people have no loyalty to anyone they only desire the delights of this world. Qaeda and its affiliates are only interested in inheriting power even if that means they have to use Iran as its logistical, moral and financial support.

Iran with its porous borders and its idolatrous statues has never interested these terrorist organisations. Why? The reason is simple since they are common terrorists and learn from each other, share intelligence, give support and spread evil. These organisations can only be defeated if their mother is eliminated. Here is a truth that for many it is bitter to swallow. Yet the facts speak for themselves.

Osama Bin Ladin was in direct contact with the Iranian Rulership, they supported him while he was alive by providing logistical support to him and financial support also to cause chaos in Afghanistan and Pakistan. To weaken their neighbors was the only way to relatively increase their own strength. So they are at war with all the countries in their neighborhood in order to dominate, oppress, seize land and they have ambitions to rule over the Arabs in particular and the Muslims in general and so on. There was an intense well documented difference between the former Al-Qaeda leader of Iraq namely Zarqawi who rightly blamed the Iranian regime for the bloodshed of the Sunni's in Iraq. And this religious cleansing is taking place to this date where the innocent Sunnis are persecuted in wholesale fashion on the behest of the pro-Iranian agents and the Shia clergy of Iraq. However Osama declared that the deaths of the Sunnis in Iraq are bearable and this is a price worth paying in exchange for Iranian support in Afghanistan. This is the politics of a betrayer to his country, his religion and a person who has the heart of a devil. The Terrorists from Al Qaeda and co and the Iranian Shia Revolutionaries carry the same traits which are they lack principles, lack truthfulness, are liars, killers of innocent people, merciless to everyone who opposes them, and hypocrites in their actions.

The political umbrella of these terrorist organisations which are operating out of Iraq,

Syria and Afghanistan is the newly declared terrorist organisations commonly known as the Islamic Brotherhood or Jamati Islami in the Indian Subcontinent.

Even after the death of Osama bin Ladin, the Iranian regime offered the family of Osama the Worlds Most wanted man, the no 1 terrorist, asylum in Iran. Many of Osama's family members including his sons have a very close relationship with Iran.

Political ideology of Iran and the status of the clergy.

Iran is a theocracy, it is ruled by the worse people of the society and this ultimately leads to evil actions. The clergy of the Iranian regime are liars and they are masters in deception. The first thing that should be made explicitly clear to the reader is that the Iranian clergy has absolutely no relationship with Islam, or the Muslim world. Their ascription is a deception to forward their own independent theology commonly known as Shites. The clergy is corrupt in every sense of the word. They have deceived their own population into believing they are pious which is far from the truth. Since the clergy is engaged in every immoral act possible whether it is legalization of fornication or killing innocent children and women or usurping the wealth of the expatriates.

At the top of **Iran's** governing structure is the Supreme Leader, Ayatollah Ali Khamenei, who succeeded Ayatollah Ruhollah Khomeini, the founder of the **Iranian** Revolution, upon

Khomeini's death in 1989. Khomeini and Khamenei are the only two men to have held the office since the establishment of the Islamic Republic in 1979. And these two men are the worse of the Iranians ever born in the last century. They have contributed to worldwide terrorism in a scale surpassing all of the other terrorists groups combined. With so much innocent bloods on the hands of these two criminals, it is only a matter of time before this regime collapses and Iran is liberated from Satan.

Criminal Iranian interference with the different countries of the world.

In the following passage we will look at the negative Iranian influence in all the countries that Iran has unilaterally interfered in. This type of unwanted interference has resulted in the deaths of many many innocent people. Nations has been torn apart and killing is rife in all the countries where Iran has interfered. The destruction in any of the countries is correlated to the strength and magnitude of the Iranian interference. So for example Iran spent in excess of $100 billion in Syria and the result is the death of more than 600,000 lives.

Afghanistan.

The nation which has contributed the most to the destruction of Afghanistan is the evil Iranian regime, it has actively poisoned the youth through its academic institutions which are primarily setup to attack the true Islaam and to propagate a terrorist mentality and methodology by converting the students to follow the pro-terrorist Iranian ideology which encourages the killing of its own people. Secondly it has aided the opponents of the official Afghanistan government by providing them with weapons and financial assistance to fight against the Afghanis. The only solution for Afghanistan is to turn away from Iran otherwise it will be weakened politically and ideologically. Politically it will be an isolated nation as many of the advanced countries led by Saudi Arabia have totally freed themselves of this evil Iranian regime. So therefore for Afghanistan to side with a weak evil country will contribute to its instability. The Iranians are only interested in pushing their own agenda in Iran similar to what they have done in Yemen, Lebanon, Syria and Iraq. So Afghanistan should refer back to the Saudi led coalition to fight this hypocritical enemy which has many faces but only one aim which is to destroy the Muslim country of Afghanistan. The wise leaders of Afghanistan will see the reality of this evil regime and the deception has been unveiled in front of the world. The crimes of the Iranian Regime have reached unprecedented levels where being patient with them is no longer a valid option. Because evil and destruction will only increase if the World Bodies are negligent and do not back the Saudi led peace initiatives. Peace can only be attained by total dismantling the Iranian apparatus from top to bottom. The Afghan political leaders have consistently argued that Iran has profited from the instability in

Afghanistan and a major factor in the cause of insecurity. The wise rulers need to replicate the Saudi government model in order to achieve real security and prosperity. The earlier it is actualized the better for the Afghan population whom has suffered for decades by the various betraying parties.

Pakistan

With respect to Pakistan, Iran has been rather more deceptive as it is aware that Pakistan is much stronger than Afghanistan so the same policies cannot be employed there. However the deception still continues through so called charitable fronts where Iran is actively trying to strengthen the Shia minority in Pakistan. They have infiltrated into the ranks of many important public institutions thus able to determine and influence many official policies. But while Pakistan is focused on the Kashmir front against the aggressor India, the Iranian border is much more of an imminent threat. Pakistan needs to redirect its resources to the Baluchistan border areas where Iran alongside Indian is behind the illegitimate Bulloch rebellion. This threat has to be eliminated and perhaps as Sadaam realised all of the Arabs will help if Pakistan was to face Iran and defeat it in totality. This is a big possibility since Pakistan Army is close to the Saudi led coalition. This is one solution where Pakistan can restore its honour and economically win many benefits. To mention just one of the Iranian aggressions which took place inside Pakistan is the incident in 1988 whereby Iranian backed delegation carried out the first suicidal mission inside

Pakistan in the city of Lahore. The target was the illustrious scholar Ihsan Ilahi Zahir who survived the bomb blast while giving a public sermon however he later succumbed to his injuries in the city of Riyadh, Saudi Arabia. Those with them on the public stages were the leaders of the Ahle Hadith faction whom have been historically pro-Saudis and were killed. It should be noted that the Shia of Pakistan are mentally programmed to be pro-Iranian and they have no loyalty to the Pakistani state. These people are betrayers and some are guilty of treason those who bypassed the official Pakistani government guidelines and went to Syria to participate in the killings of children and women at the behest of the Iranian government. Security can never be achieved in Pakistan as long as there is any type of Iranian influence, whether it is cultural, educational, politically or religious Shite ties. To achieve even partial security, Pakistan army has to get rid of all the pro-Iranian political parties and its wings.

Morocco

Recently it has been proven that the Iranian regime sent its "Hezbollah" militiamen to give arms training to the so called Polisario Front separatists those whom have illegitimately revolted against the state without any justification. Hezbollah Military officers traveled to Tindouf camps in Algeria to provide military training in using SAM-9 and anti-aircraft missiles. This has been documented and narrated by the official sources within Morocco and the Foreign Minister Bourita affirmed that the Iranian Ambassador will be expelled and the Moroccan Ambassador will be withdrawn. So the diplomatic and the economic ties have been cut with this evil criminal regime that is responsible for the killings of millions of innocent lives in Syria and Iraq. Hezbollah is the military arm of this evil Iranian regime and they have provided logistical and strategic support to the separatists namely the Polisario Front. The actions of this rogue state of Iran clearly demonstrate its intent to attack the territorial integrity of Morocco and to weaken it structurally. However Morocco has correctly aligned itself with Saudi Arabia and the rest of the Arab states by sending a clear signal to Tehran that it is unwanted and is an insignificant lowly treacherous country.

Iraq

Iran fought a fierce war with Saddam's Iraq in the 1980s and it incurred a heavy loss which exposed its weak army and weak infrastructure. The war almost lasted 10 years and Iran was humiliated by the Iraqi army. After the downfall of the Iraqi Baath Regime it allowed Iran to re-enter into Iraq politically and militarily. Iran wanted revenge so it started to train the Shia Militia to murder, kill, and shoot the Iraqi Sunni civilians. Iran promoted hatred and destabilized the country which eventually led to a civil war with many different factions including the Shia, Kurds, Sunni tribes and pro-Iranian ISIS. Iran committed innumerable war crimes in Iraq and continues to do so by using its Revolution Guard in combination with Shia cleric Sadr militias.

Iran has financially benefitted from the Iraqi destabilization and any sanctions against Iran should apply to all those regimes that continue to trade with this rogue terrorist nation. So even if Iran is put under sanctions it will not achieve the desired result unless the Iraqi regime ceases to co-operate with the Iranians. After the destabilization of Iraq, the Iraqi government is paying the Iranians for its security and there is a lot of intra-trade between the two neighbors.

Currently the Iraqi security, economy and assets are in the hands of Iran whom continue to oppress the minorities of Iraq. Iran has overtaken Iraq in its entirety; this is the reality which cannot escape anyone.

Syria

The dire situation in Syria is known to all, where genocide has been committed by the Shia ruling regime which is close to the Iranians. Iran offered them tactical support, military support and financial support to undertake a genocide on a major scale. More than half of the Syrian population has been displaced and millions have been killed. All the killings happened with the explicit approval and help of the evil Iranian regime. Bashar ideological beliefs are the same as Iran and he carries the exact same vision. So this is a clear warning to the residents of Iran that they will meet the same fate from their government if they dare to oppose the enforced

Shia ideology. The Shia ideology is totally based on oppression, this is the root of the Iranian regime and the people are only with them through fear and not love. No Iranian of any intellect has any love or loyalty for this rogue nation but is silenced due to the fear of the establishment. The regime holds many innocent prisoners whom they arrogantly punish them in public. But know that any form of oppression is limited and this cannot continue indefinitely. The oppressor will soon come to his reckoning and face justice. So indeed after the Iranian regime afflicted regional-wide atrocities its agenda has been exposed, the world has united, the deception of the Satan has been discovered. The end of this regime along with Bashar, the Houthis, Party of Satan (Hezbollah) is very near. The Iranians know they are inherently weak and they have fear casted into their hearts. They can never face the Saudis who are aided by Allaah and then the rest of the Muslim world and the rest of the world. The Saudis have a system which is based on the principles of justice thus establishing security of the highest degree. The corrupt Muslim Brotherhood group was also exposed playing contradictory politics on the one hand its shows the world it is against the Bashar regime while backing some of the notorious terrorists groups such as Daesh. And on the other hand is a stern defended of Iran, the exact enemy who facilitated the genocide in Syria. So it is apparent to all, the Muslim Brotherhood is a corrupt group aligned with the Shia Terrorists and the Takfeeri Terrorist groups. Every nation should designate them and their leaders as terrorists if they are truly against terrorism in word and deed.

Iran has greatly profited from the war in Syria, it has geopolitically, militarily, economically and ideologically gained from Syria. Prior to the war, Syria was an independent country with limited trade and co-operation with the Iranian regime. Now with Bashar with serious weakness, this has been exploited by Iran whom has managed to have a firm grip over everything in Syria. The power is in the hands of the Iranian regime who have invested heavily in Syria to strengthen the government of Bashar. Evil regimes have common ground so Iran being the most evil helps another equally corrupt and evil regime to stay in power.

Iran has in total spent in excess of $100 Billion on Syria to keep Bashar in power. This has allowed Iran to secure lucrative contracts in the Energy sectors where Iran will provide electricity, and also allowed Iran to establish a major GSM mobile company to take care of the telecommunications. Also it is responsible for the mining and agriculture of Syria where it has acquired thousands of acres of agricultural land. Also exceptions have been made for the Iranians to buy real estate and to build Shite temples and Shrines to cement the sectarian divide and change the demographics in favour of the Shite minority. "Hezbollah" families have moved into Damascus and other cities to consolidate the power and to keep Iranian interests active. Iran has exported its revolutionary principles which will further corrupt the Syrian regime and sink them more. They are totally hijacked by the Iranians and now have very limited power. The Iranians have also unified its militias which came from Pakistan, Afghanistan, Iraq and Lebanon. They also have control over the Syrian airports and have a strong military bases which potentially can overthrow Bashar when he becomes useless to them. Since this war is one of betrayal, so the betrayers will get betrayed too.

This is the general story of the Iranian regime style of doing business. It can only compete by initiating war, killing innocent people and robbing the country. These are the methods of the criminals.

Lebanon

Iran has totally held Lebanon hostage by using the party of Satan "Hezbollah" militia. This group of killer's real aim is to politically align Lebanon with Iran by any means necessary. So therefore they have infiltrated all the government institutions in order to achieve this .This cancer has prevented Lebanon to progress and Lebanon needs to fight against this cancer or it will follow the same fate as Syria and Iraq. Anyone, who aligns themselves with this evil Iranian regime, will soon or later inevitable fall backwards, the only one to profit from this human tragedy is Iran since it has partially achieved its ultimate goal which is the killing of the Sunni population. With the weakened Sunni population this is fertile ground for Iran to dominate. The only mighty country that stands in its treacherous path is Saudi Arabia and its allies whom will take the fight to Iran.

Jordan

Jordan is a firm supporter of Saudi Arabia and has taken the same stance against Iran by withdrawing its Ambassador and condemning Iran for its interference in the affairs of the Arab countries. This shows that Iran has no support except by similarly minded corrupt governments whom are only have financial interests and not humanitarian concerns.

Egypt

When the Muslim Brotherhood ruled Egypt for 1 year and then were overtaken in the same manner that they came to power, that is by way of the street protests. In the one year they ruled they literally destroyed the economy and also were aiding in the destruction of the security hence the members of the Muslim Brotherhood being convicted of treason and betrayal. In that single year they gave Iran full open access to Egypt to corrupt the country and build pro-Iranian centers which would then be the future base to undermine the Egyptian security apparatus. They did not get too far as the Army overtook power from Morsi who has publicly humiliated for his crimes against the state. So Egypt survived the Iranian threat which was facilitated by the corrupt Muslim Brotherhood.

Saudia Arabia

In Saudi Arabia, the heart of the Muslim world, the country where every Muslim is naturally affiliated with, the country for which every Muslim will fight for in order to protect the Haramain(Makkah and Madinah). However for Iran it is the complete opposite it is the no 1 enemy, they shout slogans against Saudi after the prayers, on the streets and in the parliament house. They curse the Saudi government and its wise scholars. So this is clear evidence for a person of intellect that Iran is the enemy of the Muslims. Who else would dare to say "I want to destroy Saudia". Iran has backed every terrorist residing in the Kingdom of Saudi Arabia and when the top domestic terrorist Nimr Al-Nimr was executed. Consequently the Iranian regime with the help of its mob stormed and attacked the Saudi Embassy in Tehran. These criminals had no respect for diplomatic norms or human values.

Nimr Al-Nimr studied "terrorism" in Iran and then came back to Saudi Arabia where he executed his terrorist knowledge. He used to give fiery speeches inciting the public to revolt against the authorities. His protests against the government in the city of Qatif in the year 2011 led to the deaths and injury of many police officers. He wanted a military uprising against the governments of the Gulf whom he accused of blasphemy. He was a separatist with the same agenda as the Al-Qaeda terrorists and hence met the same fate when he was executed alongside approx. 50 other terrorists from Daesh and al-Qaeda. He was guilty of sedition and treason and was funded by the Iranians who wanted to use this evil person to destabilize the Gulf countries. Despite his well-known and documented crimes the Iranian regime supports him and his followers.

In 1996 the Iranians with their proxy militia group, the Party of Satan "Hezbollah" carried out a bombing in the city of Khobar, Saudi Arabia near the Saudi military bases and the Aramco HQ. This resulted in many deaths and in 2006, a U.S. court found Iran and Hezbollah guilty of orchestrating the attack. The American judge also concluded that the attack had been approved by Iran's Supreme Leader, Ali Khamenei. So this proves that the Iranian regime from the very top is corrupt and of evil nature. The number of bombs they have attempted is innumerable and occasionally they get the odd success. However it is apparent they are very determined and focused to attack Saudi

Arabia.

Kuwait

Iran has shown its hypocrisy to Kuwait when it betrayed the good-will of the Kuwaitis whom had invited the Iran head to Kuwait and conducted business with them. At the same time there was an active Iranian backed "Hezbollah" spy cell operating from the Iranian embassy in Kuwait whom had successfully smuggled a lot of weapons through boats into Kuwait. When the Kuwaiti security forces realised the Iranians involvement in destabilizing they intended to arrest the culprits however the Iranian embassy arranged them to be smuggled out of the country via boats to Iran. The confiscated weapons were 24 hand grenades, 65 guns, 56 RPGs and 144kg of bomb-making material inside the cache in the Abdali farm. This is blatant transgression and hypocrisy showing the true nature of this evil, despicable regime that has no morality or sound vision.

Bahrain

In Bahrain Iran has meddled into the affairs for a very long time actively trying to sow the seeds of discord and anarchy. Bahrain has a government which is affording the rights of all its residents and national. There is no doubt that the Shia population of Bahrain for living in better conditions then the Shia elite in Iran. However this Satanic Iranian regime wants to incite the Shia of Bahrain so that they end up in prison by violating the laws of the country. So the Iranian regime in actuality wants to increase its borders and make illegal territorial gains through its sectarian agenda.

Qatar

Qatar although has zero Shia population has not experienced the evil designs of the Iranian regime I.e. that of incitement. Secondly the clergy of Qatar is from the terrorist Muslim Brotherhood group which gave birth to Al-Qaeda, ISIS and Nusrah. Therefore due to this the Qatar establishment has been deceived by this terrorist group and aligned itself with Iran and boycotted the Arab countries. Until one does not realise the deception of the Muslim Brotherhood then he will no doubt be deceived by the Iranian regime. The Muslim Brotherhood figures like the Egyptian Mufti Qardawi who is currently based in Doha are pro-Iranian and they are explicit supporters of the terrorist organisations. To Qardawi the genocide in Syria is a price worth paying if in return he gets the surety from Iran that it will provide logistical support to the terrorists operating in the different countries. Qardawi has betrayed his religion, his country of birth and the Arabs in general. This is why the Muslim Brotherhood is commonly referred to as The Bankrupt Brotherhood or the Brotherhood of Betrayers. The Qataris should accept the evidences against these terrorist regimes since ultimately these groups have no principles and will eventually turn against the Qatar. Muslim Brotherhood meetings and discussions only focus on one issue which is overthrowing governments by any means necessary. So anyone who does not agree with them is a legitimate target for them.

UAE

The UAE has also been a victim of Iranian aggression and Iran has illegal ceased some of the UAE Islands. They have not shown any willingness to solve the issue amicably. And these are all signs of its evil designs to advance its territorial areas.

Yemen

In Yemen the Iranians for a longtime have supported the separatist terrorist Shia group known as the Houthis. These war criminals have killed many innocent children and women in Yemen. Iran has shipped full cargo of weapons some of them are Rocket launchers and Missiles which have the ability to strike Riyadh. So this proves that Iran is at war with the heart of the Muslim world. The Iranians shamelessly attacked the Holiest place in Islam, the city of Makkah. They wanted to invade Saudi Arabia but take control of Makkah Al-Mukarramah and Madinah. The Houthis of Yemen who are funded by the Iranians are fighting the legitimate official government of Yemen. So the same cycle is repeating itself that the Iranians are exporters of terrorism and add fuel to the fire. Wherever they go they spread killings and chaos and break down the security. The Houthis are suffering on every front, but their Iranian masters are not showing any mercy to them.

Sudan

USA

Iran wishes to divert attention from its own crimes against the Muslim and push the blame onto other countries. It has for the last few decades groomed its population with the slogan "Death to America". The justification is that American has killed innocents in Iraq, Afghanistan and elsewhere. While this is not denied by any person of truth, the reality is that Iran has been a lot more detrimental to the cause of the Muslims and has the audacity to kill Muslims on a greater scale. Iran has killed innocent Muslim civilians in Yemen, Syria, Lebanon, and Iraq and inside Iran itself. Furthermore it has poisoned their minds to adopt a satanic ideology which is complete betrayal to their religion, to their country and to themselves. This Satanic Ideology is what is commonly referred to as Khomeinism.

The USA has rightly imposed trade sanctions on Iran but this is not enough it is not yielding the desired result since the Iranians have an escape route via Iraq. Countries who continue to trade with Iran also should be met with US trade sanctions thus compelling them to choose either trade with USA or Iran.

UK

The UK is politically weak due to its so called democratic parliament which is in a status of confusion. Everything is debatable even though the issue may be extremely clear and demanding immediate action. The hesitance of the UK government to take any type of action against the Iranians will be detrimental to the UK's economy since the nations united against Iran will not give it any trade preferential contracts. At the same time the UK will not gain anything from a falling Iranian regime so perhaps the UK should re-evaluate its policies and morality.

France

Fatwa against Rushdie

In 1989 Khomeini issued a fatwa against the relatively unknown Indian British author Rushdie which was in reality an order to kill him. It was said that the fatwa was stated due to the blasphemous content of Rushdie Book Satanic

Verses. It is true that the book like many others found in the secular Western universities has falsehood and blasphemy against the Prophets, in particular the final Messenger of Allaah may the peace and blessings of Allaah be upon him. But for Khomeini this was a public stunt and he wanted to show the Muslims that he is concerned about this blasphemy. However the reality is that the Shia has the most blasphemous books ever written against Islaam and its final Prophet may the peace and blessings of Allaah be upon him. Khomeini himself has authored many blasphemous books against Islaam which insult the Prophets, the Companions of the Prophet Muhammad May the peace and blessings of Allaah be upon him. So this deed of his was a complete contradiction and was done with the intent to deceive the common Muslims that Iran is concerned with the affairs of the Muslims. However, in reality let it is known that Iran is the biggest threat to the Muslim world, since it aims to poison the Muslims from within by deceiving them. The external enemy can never achieve what the internal unperceived enemy can achieve. Iran is an enemy not just to the people of the Middle East or South Asia but an enemy to their belief system. The war against Iran is a war against evil. Iran has pure hypocrisy in the true meaning of the word. Hypocrisy in its beliefs and in its actions, they have no truthfulness with them whatsoever. Iran is the axis of evil.

Palestine issue.

Similarly with regards to the Palestine cause Iran has exploited this to its advantage. The Iranian regime main aim is to kill and completely annihilate the Sunni and overtake their territories. So why would Iran support the Palestinians? The reality is that it doesn't support them but only deceive them through buying out the Hamas leadership. The evil Iranians know that Hamas doesn't have the military capability to challenge Israel whom has mercilessly killed the Palestine for many decades. So if there is any military capability and no back up support either then why goes to a war which you will only loose and the general civilian populations will suffer. The end result in such a scenario is that many innocent deaths will occur as is evident from the last few years. It is the Sunni blood which is spilt which makes the

Iranians happy and their aims have been fulfilled. As for Hamas they carry a terrorist ideology and have betrayed the Muslims by aligning himself with the prime enemy of the Muslims those who have killed more Muslims than any other foreign country in the last 20 years. With the killings of the innocent Palestinians the Hamas profit by taking charity from all over the world. This cycle is repeated every year with the same result. The deluded ones think that Iran is sympathetic and has brotherly relations with the Palestine however this is only a myth and the reality is the exact opposite.

Corruption

Ali Khamenei is a brutal ruler of Iran, who is a rich autocrat having acquired ill-gotten wealth in excess of $95 billion. This makes him one of the richest people in the world; he is the head of the Setad group of companies. These companies are the forefront of international corruption by providing logistical and military support to the Iranian backed militias worldwide. Foreign firms need to be cautious when doing business with Iranian regime because they are corrupt and will not honour any agreements once the sanctions are back in place.

Nuclear deal

There is a lot of recent controversy around the nuclear deal with Iran. However the facts clearly indicate that this has been detrimental to the regional security and accelerated the Iranian regime willingness to destabilize the other countries in the region. This has ultimately led to war and suffering on a grand scale. This is only natural that one the Iranians had access to money and financial services they would sponsor their no 1 export which is none other than terrorism. They have the largest terrorist network in the world, militias in all the countries actively plotting bombs and providing financial aid. When the Iranian regime was under sanctions it was not able to provide financial help on such a scale as was possible after the Nuclear deal. With restricted financial power this also translated to less military assistance and hence less killings and less terrorism.

The Nuclear deal has caused the following; these are facts which are not challenged:

i) Nuclear deal means more money for Iran through open markets to sell oil and gas. With more money means more assistance for the Militias and military weapons. With more weapons it will be inevitably result in more terrorism and killings.

ii) It has increased the investments of Iranian in Syria whose sole aim is to strengthen Bashar. This has ultimately led to more killings on a larger scale.

iii) Iran has been able more to provide military assistance and high value weapons to the Houthis of Yemen which has ultimately led to more killings and a prolonged war based on sectarian agenda of Iran.

iv) Iran has been able to establish a professional network of militias in Iraq whom have been endorsed officially by the Iraqi government and have official ranking. There are around 40 of these Shia militias who are guilty of war crimes and killings on a sectarian basis. Now these forces commonly known as the Popular Mobilization Forces are an integral part of the political and security establishment of Iraq.

v) With the nuclear deal it has allowed Iran to increase funding of its domestic security forces which as the Revolutionary Guards who are the main benefactors of the increased financial aid.

At the same time the local forces with access to more funds have been able to oppress the local population, imprison them, suppressing them and killing them. The local average Iranian has not benefitted much from this Nuclear deal.

vi) The natural rectification to this mistake is to revoke this deal and re-impose the sanctions in order to reverse these terrorist activities or to bring them down to a complete halt. The nuclear deal has given the Iranian regime legitimacy and sent a signal to the world that despite being the biggest state sponsor of terrorism it does not hinder your ability to conduct business with the leading western economies.

List of Bombings

1988 Iranian Massacre

In 1988 when the Iran-Iraq was coming to an end, and the general population had witnessed almost 10 years of government corruption, evil agenda and unjustified killings. The general word on the street was that the Iranian regime is evil, consequently the government decided to send a strong signal in order to instill the fear into the hearts of the people. Because the government knew only way to control the people is to put fear into them, this is the way of all oppressive regimes. This is the way of the criminals who frighten you, take your wealth, and kill you. So the regime killed more than 5000 people.

The killing was endorsed official by a fatwa issued by the Supreme leader Ruhollah Khomeini, who became the leader after the revolution. It was oppressive and merciless. Punishment was not proportionate to the alleged crime. Prisoners, including old men, young women and teenagers, were loaded onto forklift trucks and hanged from cranes and beams in groups of five or six at half-hourly intervals all day long. Others were killed by the Revolutionary Guards with automatic AK47's pointed directly at the skulls. Those not executed were subjected to torture. The victims were intellectuals, students, Sunnis, other opposition parties and Arab ethnic group and religious minorities. Many had initially been sentenced for non-violent offences such as distributing newspapers and leaflets, taking part in demonstrations or collecting funds for prisoners' families, according to a report published by Amnesty International, an NGO, in 1990.

The Iranians regime has not compensated anyone of the innocent people for these crimes nor been taken to account.

List of hostages

Iran Hostage crisis was a clear example that Iran does not honour its agreements and the international conventions and protocols relating to foreign diplomats. For this reason alone the Iranian regime deserves to be boycotted, as over the years they have violated all the norms. From

November 4, 1979 to January 20, 1981 a total of 52 American diplomats were taken hostage by the Iranian regime. This is a world record for the longest hostage crisis in recorded history. Iran also holds the world record for being the No 1 exporter of terrorism since 1979, a record it has held and is the undisputed champion of state sponsored terrorism.

This is typical Iranian regime policy to hold foreign hostages in order to blackmail the respective governments and buy time to implement its evil planned activities. So they have taken hostages of many Western countries over the years and this is blatant violations of agreements and criminal blackmail. This is why the Iranian regime cannot be trusted and it is headed by hardened criminals whom profit through war.

Iran admits to facilitating Visas for Al-Qaeda

Iranian TV interview conducted on the May 30, 2018 details the irrefutable links between Iran and Al-Qaeda before and after 9/11 attacks on the US and reveals Iranian immigration agreed not to stamp passports of Al-Qaeda members in transit so they would still be able to enter Saudi Arabia. This was all done with the explicit permission of the Iranian intelligence services that provided them with logistical support, financial support. Al-Qaeda members were sitting alongside Hezbollah Shia members. This is clear proof that the Al-Qaeda leadership has sold its religion and has no moral compass. You have an individual who claims he is Muslim then has the audacity to sit with those who curse the Prophets, the Companions of the Final Prophet of Allah peace and sallam be upon him.

This was the method of the Al-Qaeda leader, Osama bin Ladin who outlined the methodology the Al-Qaeda group should interact with Iran and in his 113 letters which were found on his deathbed, it proved the links with Iran and Iran being a key component for Al-Qaeda fight against Saudi Arabia. Verily the devil has deceived them they leave the clear enemies and fight their own brothers. They fight on behalf of Iran otherwise the devil Iran will never entertain them. But Al-Qaeda are fools and only interested in a few dollars.

Mohammed-Javad Larijani, the international affairs assistant in the Iranian judiciary, has revealed Iran intelligence services helped the terrorists of Al-Qaeda to pass through its territory. There is no doubt that Iran and Al-

Qaeda and its sub branches have high level contact and co-operation in terrorist activities. They are different sides to the same coin and don't forget Iran commemorated a special Coin with Syed Qutb picture upon his death. This was to honour Syed Qutb the father of the Muslim Brotherhood and revered figure for Al-Qaeda. So therefore there is historical understanding between these two evil terrorist networks to destroy the Muslim countries and the world at large.

List of diplomatic incursions

Methodology of propagating pro-Iranian propaganda.

<u>Economic sanctions</u>

Sanctions imposed by the American government is a step in the right direction, it will break the backbone of this evil regime and prevent them to export its terrorist ideology and campaign. Sanctions should also be imposed on those countries which continue to trade with Iran regardless of who that country may be. There has to be strong enforcement of these sanctions for it to be effective. Iraq also conducts most of its trade with Iran and hence should be subjected to the same sanctions.

Military solutions

if Iran does not amend its ways, then the future strategy should be for Afghanistan to start its campaign for the 2nd Jihad. And no doubt if Afghanistan can defeat the Russians who at the time had one of the strongest armies, most sophisticated weapons then Iran is a much easier task. Afghan will be assured of international support and its army will be assisted by the Muslim Military coalition.

Statement of Foreign Minister of Saudi Arabia.

The fact is that Iran is the leading state-sponsor of terrorism, with government officials directly responsible for numerous terrorist attacks since 1979. These include suicide bombings of the U.S. Embassy in Beirut and the Marine barracks at Beirut International Airport; the bombing of Khobar Towers in Saudi Arabia in 1996; attacks against more than a dozen embassies in Iran, including those of Britain, the U.S. and Saudi Arabia; and the assassination of diplomats around the world, to name a few examples.

Nor can one get around the fact that Iran uses terrorism to advance its aggressive policies. Iran cannot talk about fighting extremism while its leaders, Quds Force and Revolutionary Guard continue to fund, train, and arm and facilitate acts of terrorism.

If Iran wants to demonstrate sincerity in contributing to the global war on terrorism, it could have begun by handing over al Qaeda leaders who have enjoyed sanctuary in Iran. These have included Osama bin Laden's son, Saad, and al Qaeda's chief of operations, Saif al-Adel, along with numerous other operatives guilty of attacks against Saudi Arabia, the U.S. and other targets. It is a fact that Saif al-Adel placed a call from Iran in May 2003 giving orders for the Riyadh bombings that claimed more than 30 lives, including eight Americans. Yet he still benefits from Iranian protection.

Iran could also stop funding terrorist organizations, including Hezbollah, whose secretary-general recently boasted that his organization gets 100% of its funding from Iran. Iran could stop producing and distributing improvised explosive devices, or IEDs, which have killed or injured thousands of U.S. troops in Iraq and Afghanistan. And Iran could halt supplying weapons to terrorists and sectarian militias in the region who seek to replace legitimate governments with Iranian puppets.

In Syria, the blood of the more than 500,000

people slaughtered by the regime of Bashar al-Assad stains the hands of Iran, which sent forces—both regular troops and nonstate actors—to prop up the Syrian regime. Iranian leaders have said publicly that if not for their efforts, Assad would have fallen from power.

Iranian officials sometimes lament sectarian strife and violence. But here again, the facts are stubborn. The region and the world were at peace with Iran until the Ayatollah Khomeini's 1979 Islamic revolution, whose principal slogan remains, "Death to America!" Mullahs seized power and vowed—as written in their constitution—to export the revolution and spread their ideology through religious and sectarian conflict.

To export the revolution, Iran set up so-called Cultural Centers of the Revolutionary Guard in many countries, including Sudan, Nigeria, Syria, Lebanon, Yemen and the Comoros Islands. The aim was to spread their ideology through propaganda and violence. Iran went so far as to propagate that the Shiite Muslims living outside Iran belong to Iran and not the countries of which they are citizens. This is unacceptable interference in other countries and should be rejected by all nations.

It is this ideology of "Khomeinism"—driven by an appetite for expansion, fueled by anti-Western hatred and motivated by sectarianism—that has energized and empowered extremism. Only by ridding the world of this toxic and radical mind-set can sectarianism be contained, terrorism defeated and calm restored to the region. If Iran is serious about combating extremism, then it should refrain from policies and actions that give rise to extremism.

Since signing the nuclear deal with the U.S. last year, Iranian leaders have taken to pointing fingers at others to assign blame for the regional problems that they helped create. But before buying into their rhetoric, consider a few questions: Which country issues a fatwa for the execution of author Salman Rushdie, a death threat that is still in force today? (Iran.) What country has attacked more than a dozen embassies inside its own territory in violation of all international laws? (Iran.) What country managed, planned and executed the 1996 attack in Khobar Towers against the American Marines? (Iran.) Do these answers describe a country that is serious about combating terrorism and extremism?

The rest of the Islamic world has unanimously condemned Iran's behavior. In Istanbul in April, the Organization of Islamic Cooperation formally rejected and deplored Iran's policies of sectarianism, interference in the affairs of others and support for terrorism.

Saudi Arabia is a leader in the war against terrorism. My country brought the world together for an international conference in 2005 to align nations in the fight against terrorism. The kingdom contributed more than $100 million to create a global center for counterterrorism at the United Nations and established a 40-member Islamic Military Coalition to combat terrorism and extremism. It also is a member of the U.S.-led Global Coalition to Counter ISIL and is part of the coalition's continuing military operations.

The kingdom has also foiled several attacks aimed at the U.S., and its leaders have been a target of suicide terror attacks. The kingdom's record is clear, and attested to by our allies and the international community.

Iran's record is one of death and destruction, as the situation in Syria and parts of Iraq clearly attests. Words will not change that; concrete action will.

Saudi Arabia's position has remained constant with regard to Iran. The kingdom would welcome better relations with Iran, based on the principles of good neighborliness and noninterference in the affairs of others. That means Iran has to abandon its subversive and hostile activities and stop its support for terrorism. Thus far, Iran's record has not been encouraging.

Ref: https://www.wsj.com/articles/iran-cant-whitewash-its-record-of-terror-1474234929?utm_source=twitterfeed&utm_medium=twitter

A word of truth

Many of the biased writers in the West have incorrectly shifted some of the blame to Saudi Arabia. This is due to a combination of ignorance of the true perception of affairs and lack of investigative journalism.

To overcome the myth that many of the Saudi preachers preach pro-Muslim Brotherhood politics then this is not true. Muslim Brotherhood is officially designated as terrorist organisations. Many of those who promoted the activities of the Muslim Brotherhood or defended them they are currently jailed in the Kingdom of Saudi Arabia. This is clear proof that Saudi Arabia does not tolerate any type of terrorism activity whether it is ideological or practical engagement, whether it is inside the Kingdom or outside.

At the government level the wise rulers of Saudi Arabia are united with the true Ahlus Sunnah scholars and they do not differ on any matter with regards to how to deal with this cancer which has plagued the world. There has been a massive crackdown on all forms of terrorism and it is correct to say that Saudi has been at the forefront of this war on terrorism. Whether this terrorism was in the shape of Usama bin Ladin then the Saudi scholars condemned him, isolated him and imprisoned anyone who has remotely sympathetic towards him. Furthermore with the emergence of Daesh the Saudi state has been instrumental in dismantling them and has made great progress which is acknowledged by the whole world. In fact the Saudi reformation center for terrorists is the most successful program ever launched to tackle terrorism whereby the vast majority of those affected by the terrorist ideology (Muslim brotherhood) have retracted and repented and been successfully reintegrated into the society as productive members.

The Shariah rulings of the Saudi scholars led by the former Mufti Abdul Aziz bin Abdullah Bin Baz is all too apparent for everyone to see how far the Saudis have gone to irradiate this cancer from the roots. The former Mufti ordered the detention of the two most prominent radical callers namely Safar and Salman Al Awda as they were the heads calling to a deviant interpretation of Islaam I.e. the way of the Takfeeris. Similarly the stance they have taken against Iran is praiseworthy since Iran is the largest sponsor of terrorism worldwide. They have also taken a praiseworthy stance against Qatar who has been influenced by the Muslim Brotherhood and their head namely Yousaf

Qardawi has taken a big role in forming the foreign policies of Qatar and encouraged cooperation with the Terrorist organisations worldwide.

In Sunni mainstream Islam it is forbidden to revolt against the legitimate rulers as this causes bloodshed. Hence there is more loss then any perceived benefit of overthrowing the Ruler. Furthermore the Ruler has under his disposal the full army and the balance is his favour. It is not permissible to revolt or incite the population to rebel against the legitimate Muslim Ruler. This is the creed which is followed in Saudi Arabia and the other Muslim countries that issues are resolved through dialogue and advise without resorting to humiliating the ruler or incitement against him or taking up arms against him. However with the ISIS deviant interpretations and the Shia Iranian religion it is part of their methodology to incite the public to cause revolutions. These so called revolutions in the Arab spring did not bring any benefit to these countries rather with the dwindling security situation the economy collapses causing poverty and weakness. Iran is actively inciting the local population of the all the countries it has interfered in to rebel against the legitimate authorities , it has provided them with financial backing, military training, logistical support and a deviant satanic ideology to kill innocent people.

The Iranians have a sectarian agenda and they want to deceive the world and it should be made absolutely clear to all that mainstream

Islam which is the Sunni Islam is totally free from the misinterpretations of the Takfeeri Muslim Brotherhood and also totally different to the Iranian Shia version. In fact it is correct to say there is nothing common between the Shia Twelvers of Iran and the Mainstream Sunni Islam which is predominant in the Middle East. The Shia of Iran claim they have a different Quran and different sources of knowledge so therefore it is incorrect to classify the actions of this rogue nation as Islamic or representative of the Muslims in any capacity whatsoever. Similarly the reader should not be deceived by the pure political nature of the Muslim Brotherhood movement which has simply hijacked the Islamic religion in order to establish a platform to acquire and fulfill political aspirations of power and wealth. They also use different sources to Mainstream Islam and heavily rely on the books of Syed Qutb, Usama Bin Ladin and his likes which are in reality a total misrepresentation of true Islaam. In Saudi Arabia the methodology which is followed is that the sacred texts are interpreted as the first scholars of Islaam interpreted them and this is the actual pure Islam a religion full of mercy and compassion. The peaceful religion of Islam which has outlined the rights of all of of mankind .Islam calls them to the worship of their Creator, Sustainer and Owner. It calls them not to direct any worship to any of the creation besides the one true deity worthy of worship who is Allaah alone.

<u>Conclusion</u>

The only logical deduction after reading the evidences presented which outline the aggressive nature of the Iranian interferences in the security integrity of other nations is to take firm action. This action has to be a co-ordinated effort and Saudi Arabia which is the heart of the Muslim world has taken the initiative in this regard. Similarly the USA has acknowledged that the Saudi stance is the correct logical stance which is based on the principles of justice and truthfulness. So therefore in order to achieve this lofty goal of dismantling this terrorist network there has to be International consensus on the type of sanctions to be implemented. There has to be severe economic sanctions which should cripple the already weak economy and also punish those companies who wish to trade with this rogue nation.

Once Iran is economically defeated and deflated then the next logical step can be undertaken by the world coalition. Previous attempts to weaken the Iranian state and to punish them for their military adventurism and their military support for the terrorist proxies have failed.

Now there has to be a determined effort to exert full pressure which is consistent that causes a favorable response. The Iranian clergy who are terrorists ruling the Iranian territory need to be overcome otherwise the Middle East chaos will only increase leading to many more thousands of deaths.

The problems with Iran are on multiple levels relating to domestic oppression of a large segment of the society whom are not only denied their most basis rights but are subjected to persecution and daily humiliation at the hands of this brutal regime.

The next level is the regional issues where Iran has aggressively interfered into the security affairs of its neighbors in order to destabilize their security. Security of a nation is the most valuable asset it has and only once security is guaranteed can the residents fulfill their fundamental religious and economic needs. Iran has caused severe chaos where the end looks very bleak and remote in Syria and Iraq. Furthermore it has aided the renegade Houthi criminals in Yemen whom continue to cause bloodshed. Also similarly in Bahrain they planted the seeds of discord based on sectarian lines. In UAE they have occupied the legal territory belonging to the rightful owner, UAE.

Also on the eastern border they continue provide the Taliban logistical support to wage war against the Afghan population. They have also oppressed the Baluch nation for decades, denying them their fundamental rights and arming them to fight against the Pakistani security forces. The BLA is partially funded by Iran.

On the International level Iran claims to have achieved Nuclear capabilities which will no doubt will start the Nuclear race in order to act as deterrent for Iran to attack. Iran lacking any moral integrity and a history of violations, a dark history of killings, bombings and assassinations will resort to the nuclear option when it wants to. So therefore in order to deter this rogue nation to pursue this evil path then other nations which are threatened by Iran have the right to assume access to nuclear capabilities. The wider implications are that unless the world community agrees to tackle this issue, the problems will only increase and the price to pay will be very high later on. So therefore the wise option is to defeat this nation on all fronts, diplomatically and economically and by other means. The threat from Iran is imminent so therefore the solution has to be ready to counter this threat. The price paid in Syria is immense where Iran has ignored International conventions and regulations and aided the Syrian regime to kill their own people without any justification whatsoever. They imported paid Shia fighters from Afghanistan and Pakistan and when these fighters return back they will be an additional security threat in their respective countries.

Iran has no justification to transgress these boundaries. Iran is not a victim but an oppressor. Saudi Arabia has continually allowed the Iranians to visit Saudi Arabia and afforded them excellent services in Makkah and Madinah. But who did Iran reciprocate this gesture by encouraging Iranian protestors to attack the Saudi Embassy in Iran. They acted in a cheap gangster style fashion violating the diplomatic norms where nations ensure security is maintained for visiting diplomats and their embassies. This is the real face of Iran, it is ruled by the clergy whom have hearts of devils and their actions are evil. Barbaric Iran is responsible for the atrocities taking place in the Middle East and it should be held responsible.

Iran terrorism is collaborated with the Al-Qaeda and Daesh; the two groups may appear to divergent but in actuality for interconnected as their main aim is one. The corrupt Muslim Brotherhood is the bridge between the Shia Militias and the Takfeeri Terrorist groups such as Al-Qaeda and Daesh. So Al-Qaeda cannot be defeated unless Iran terrorism is also defeated since they take refuge in Iran and those countries which are sympathetic towards their cause such as Iraq, Lebanon and Yemen.

Iran can be defeated with the cooperation of those countries that have a border with it. It has to be liberated before further atrocities and genocides like that which took place in Syria are repeated. The criminal has been identified, now it's time to execute it as a mercy to the rest of the people whom are harmed by it on a daily basis.

Finally it is only a matter of time, that this rogue regime meets its inevitable fate of self-destruction and humiliation. Regimes which are built on the principles of oppression all eventually come to an end and history is a witness to that. So therefore Iran which has increasingly become more evil violated every moral value and continues to export its terrorist agenda worldwide will certainly fall. The darkest hours are to come and the evil leaders of this rogue regime can no longer hide their apparent crimes, nor deceive even their own population and nothing can save them from this destruction.

On the other hand , the neighbour of Iran, led by the wise Rulers of the Kingdom of Saudi Arabia have the utmost respect on the International forum, they have created an alliance of Muslim countries for military services and all of this is pressure to deflate the corrupt Iranian regime. So we will see a stronger Saudi Arabia, which represents goodness defeat the axis of evil, Iran. This is truly a war between the good (Saudi) and the evil (Iran).

Completed on

9th July 2018